The 3D Coloring Book

Bane Hurst

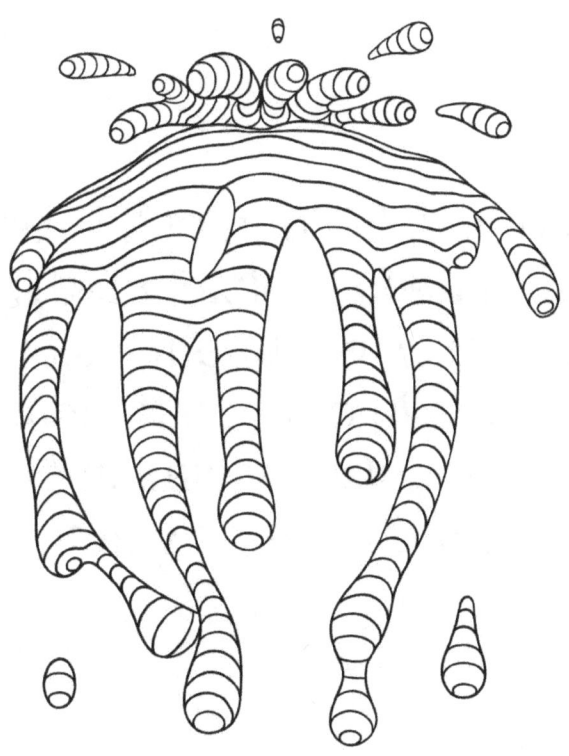

Visit *banehurst.com* for tips about
blending colors, **shading** and more!

Copyright © 2018 Bane Hurst
All rights reserved.
ISBN-13: 978-1985670358
ISBN-10: 1985670356

All rights reserved. No part of this book may be reproduced, scanned, or distributed in any printed or electronic form without permission. Please do not participate in or encourage piracy of copyrighted materials in violation of the author/illustrator's rights. Purchase only authorized editions.

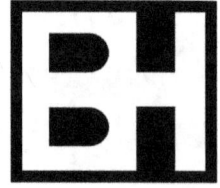

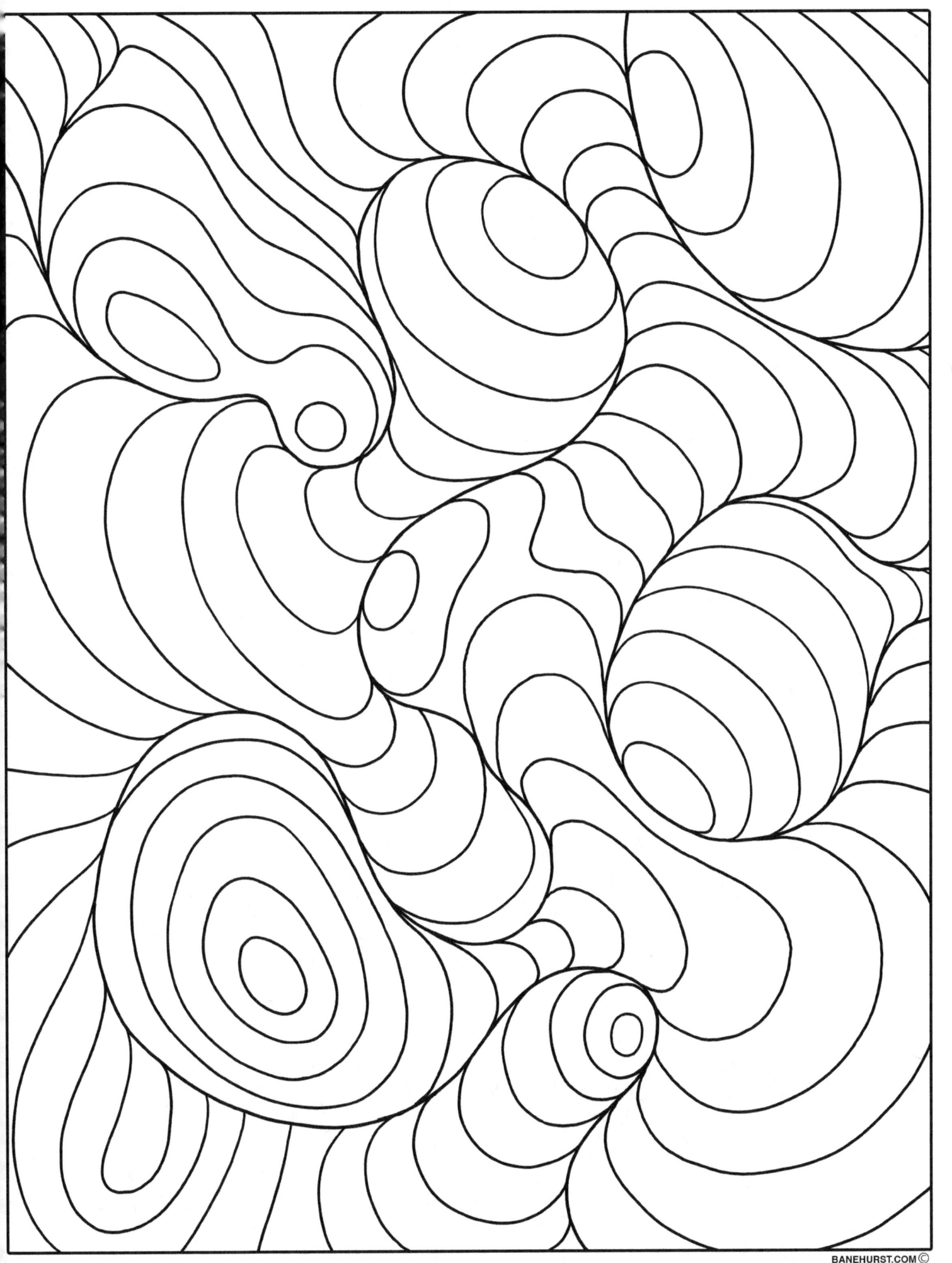

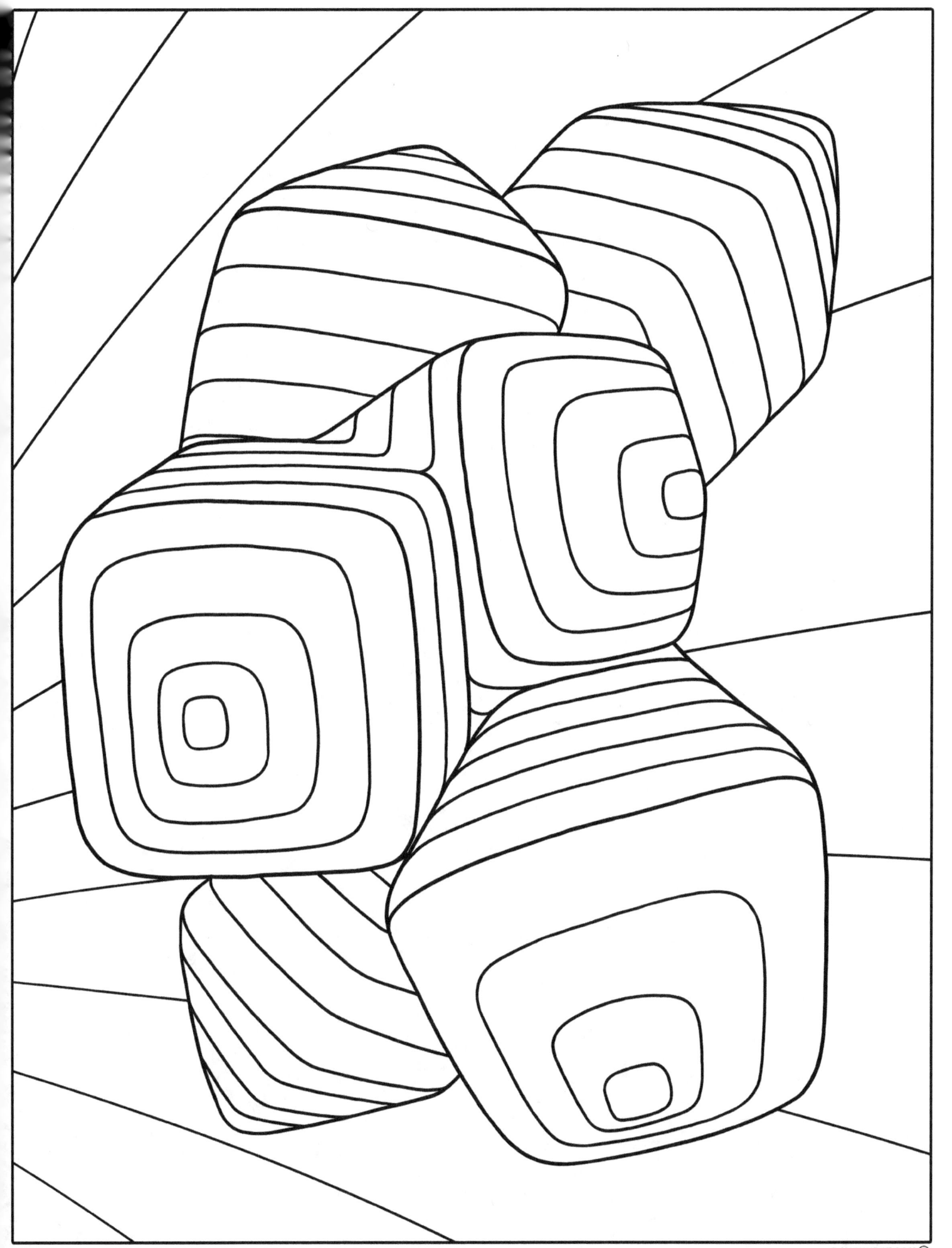

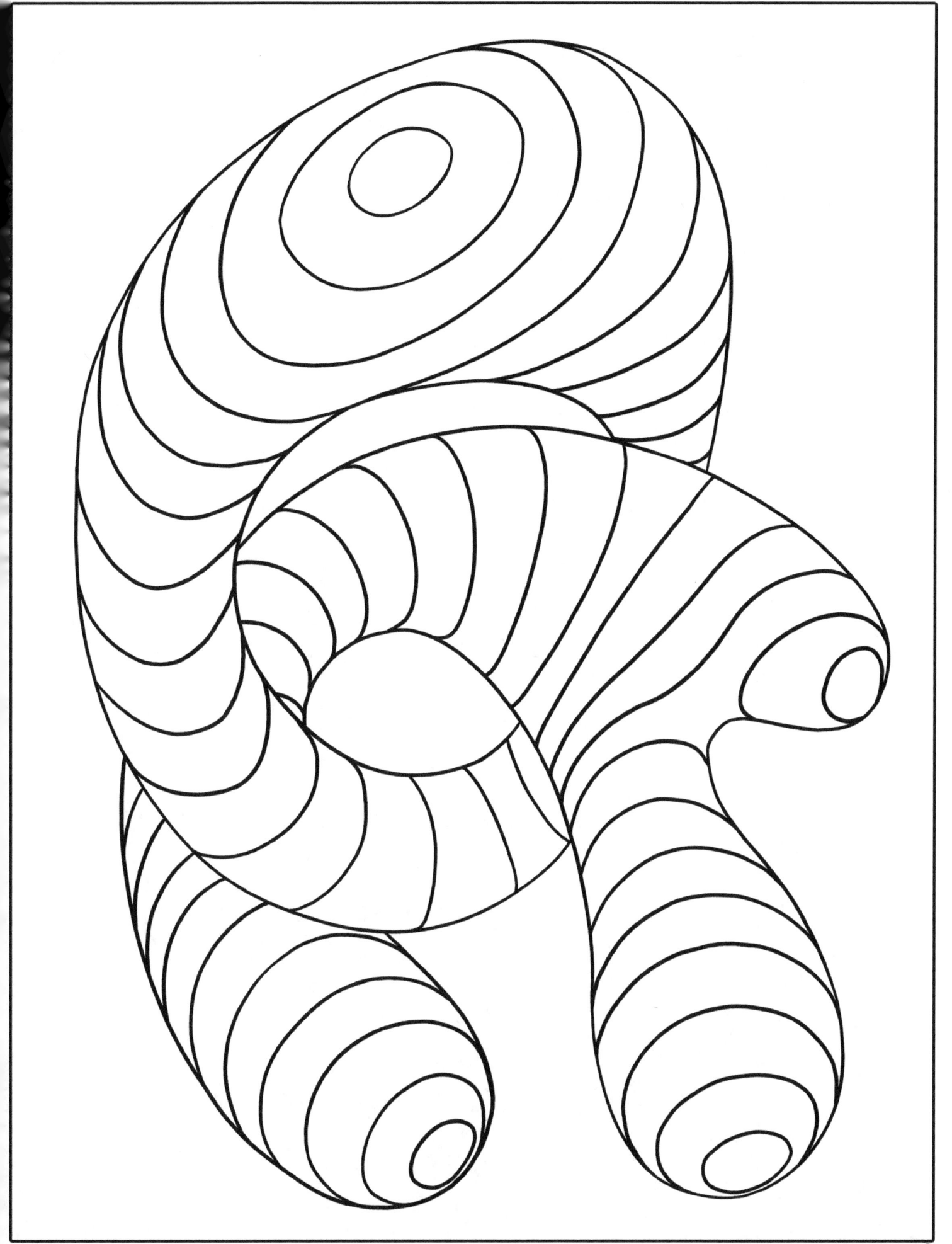

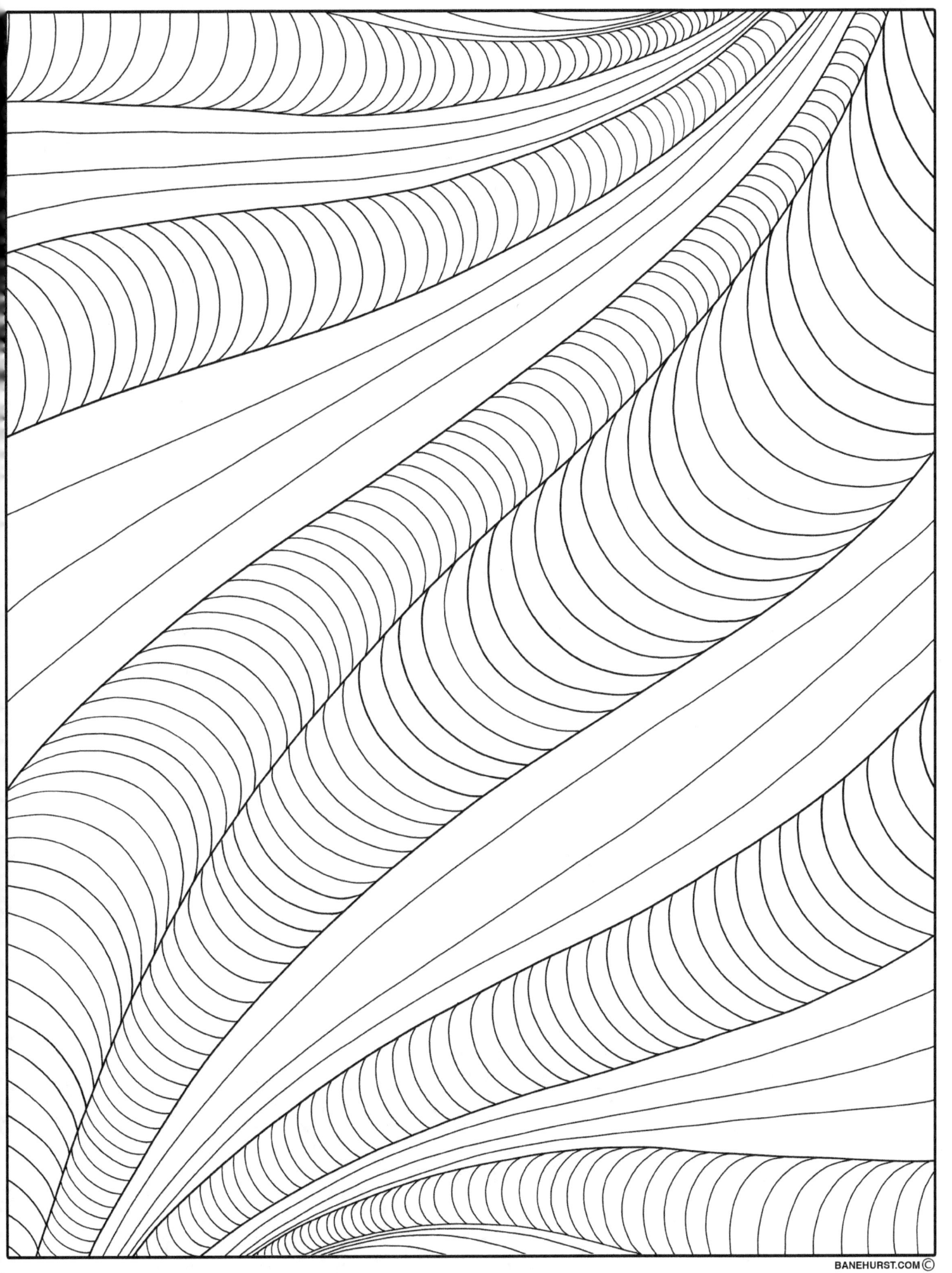

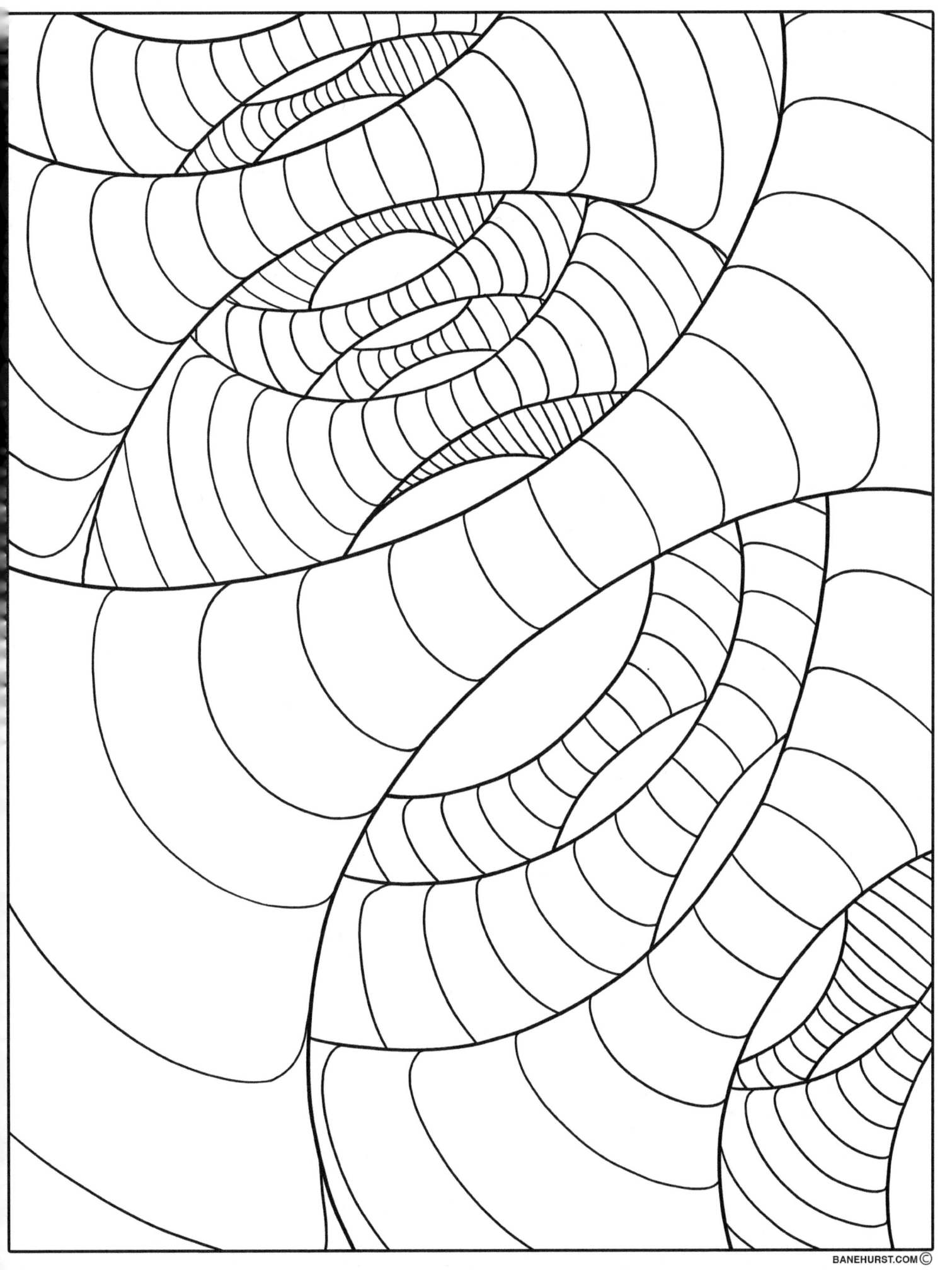

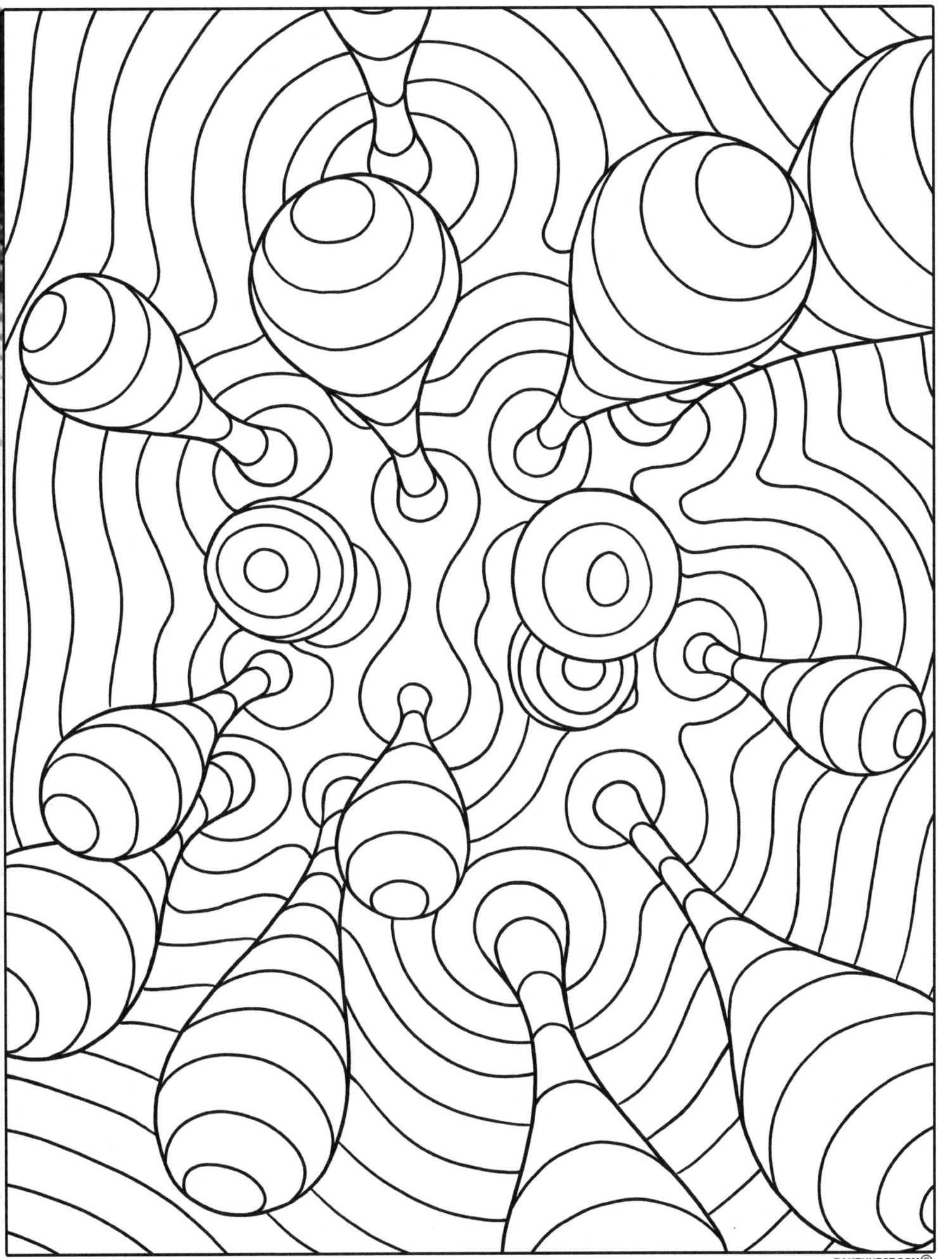

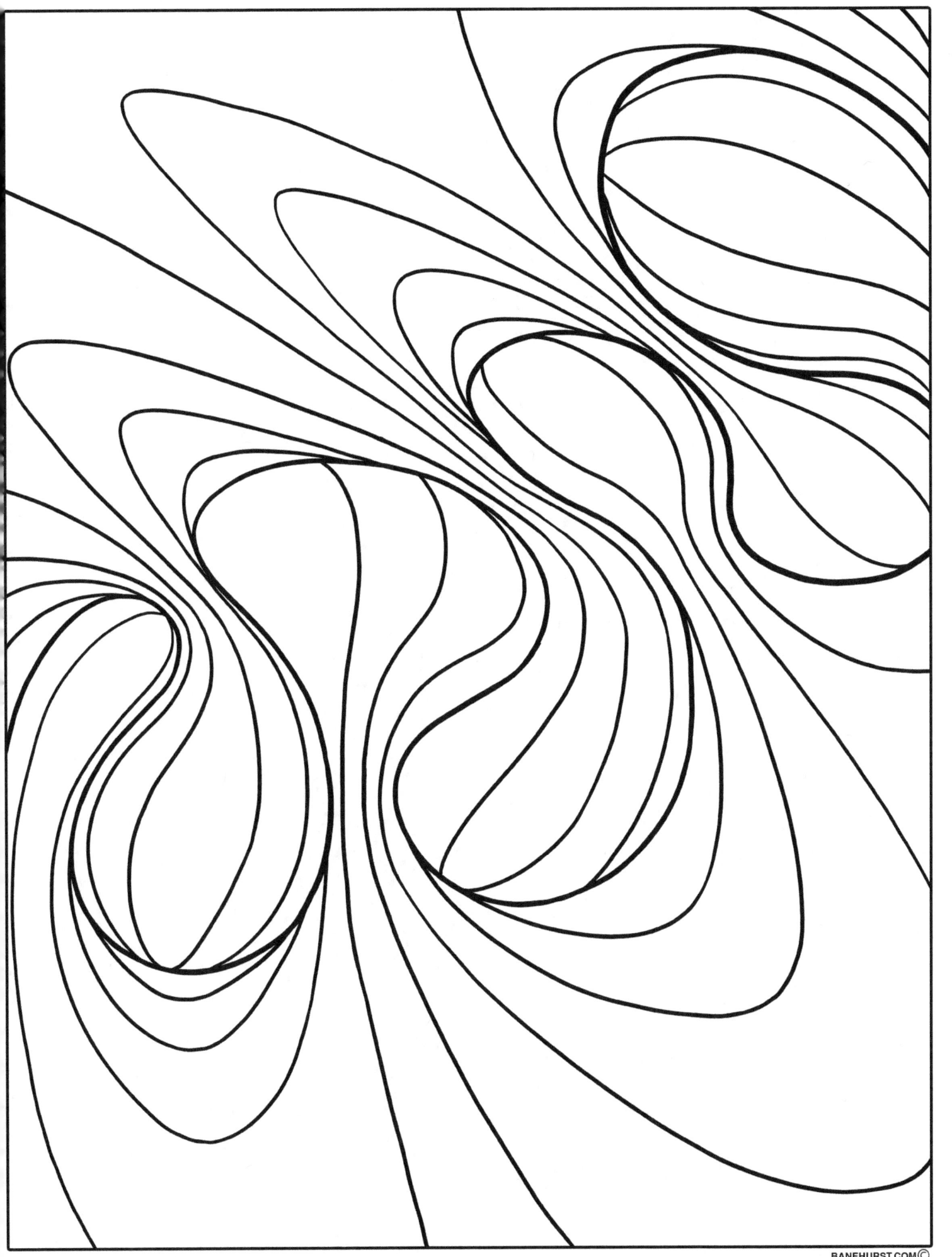

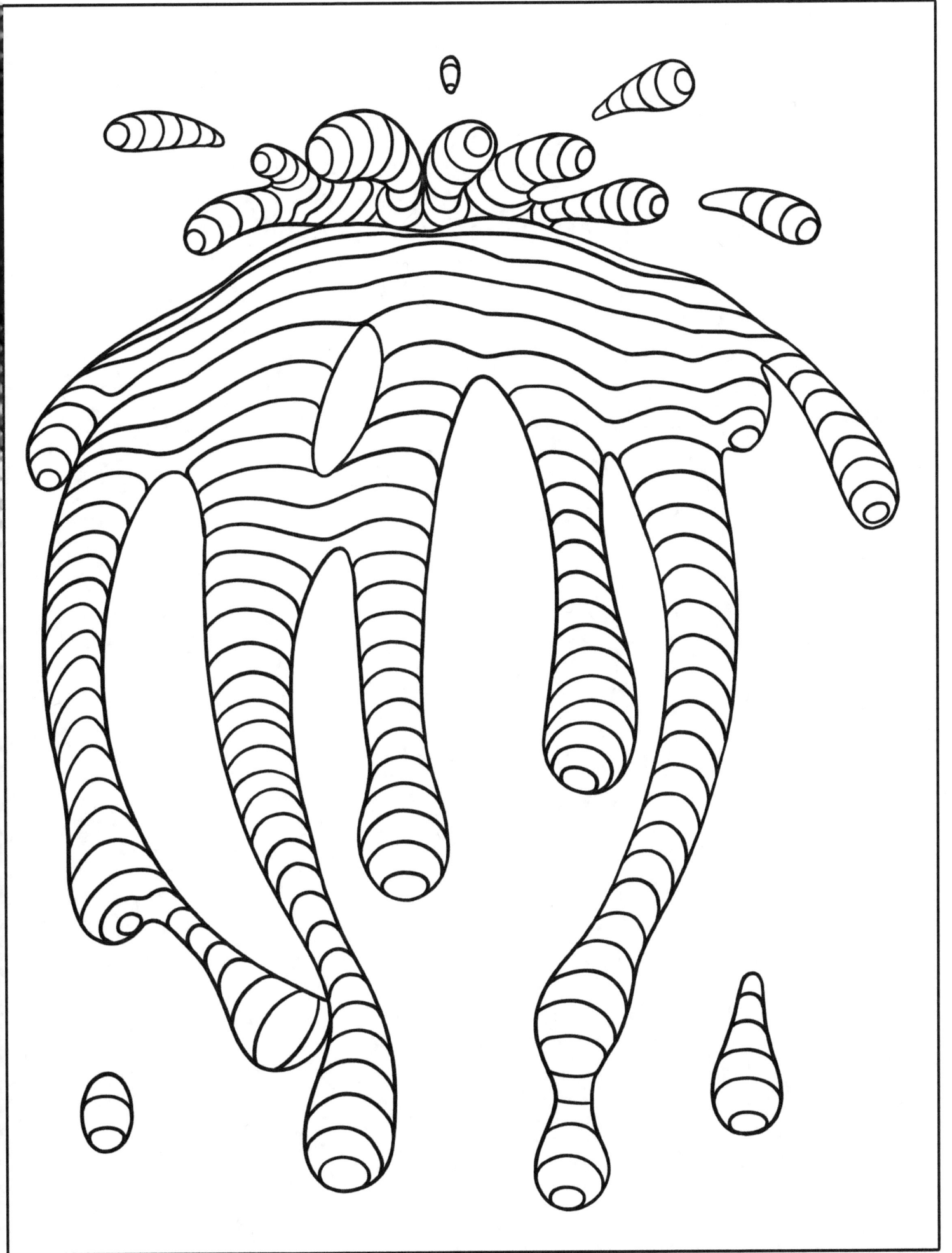

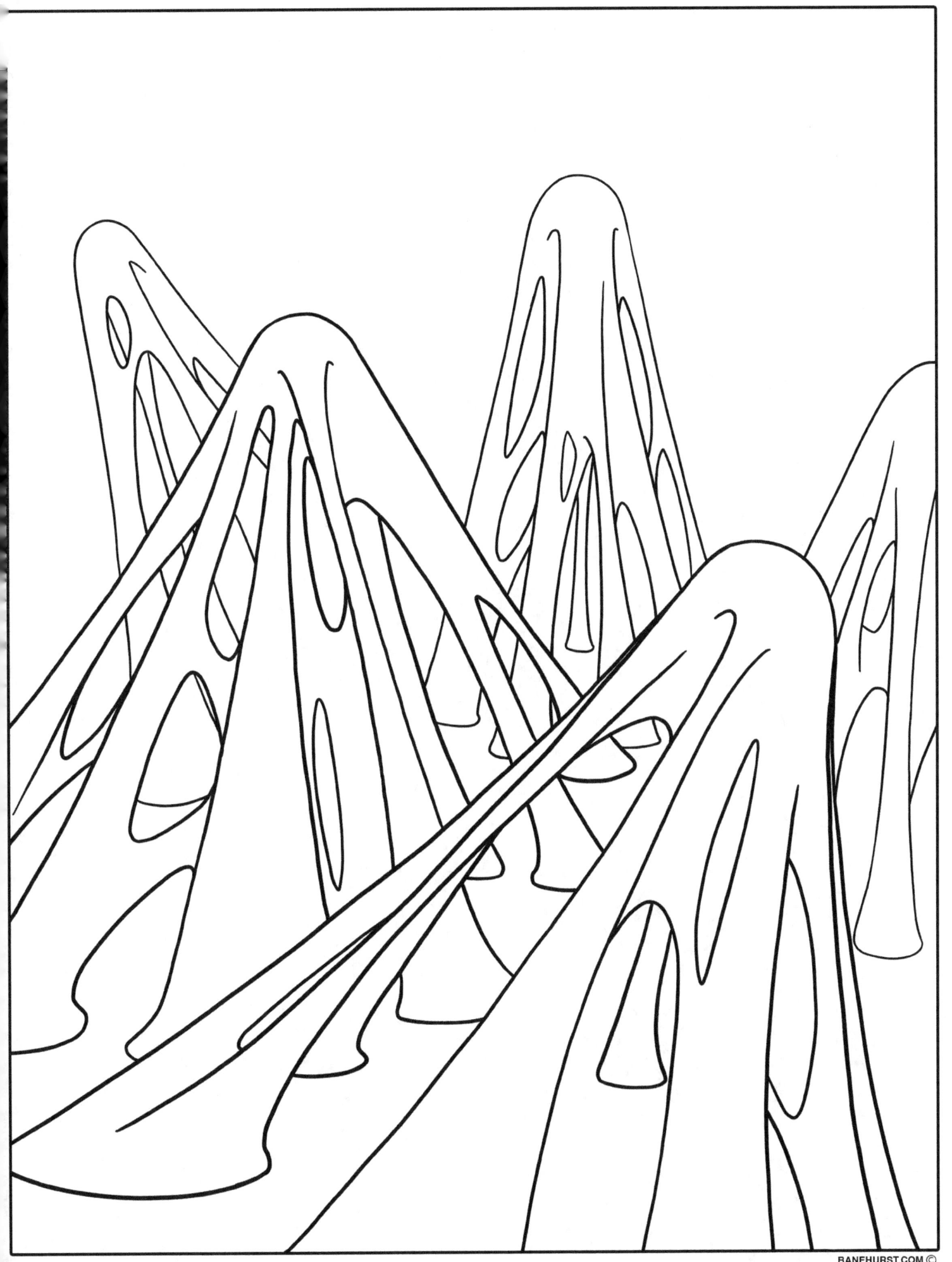

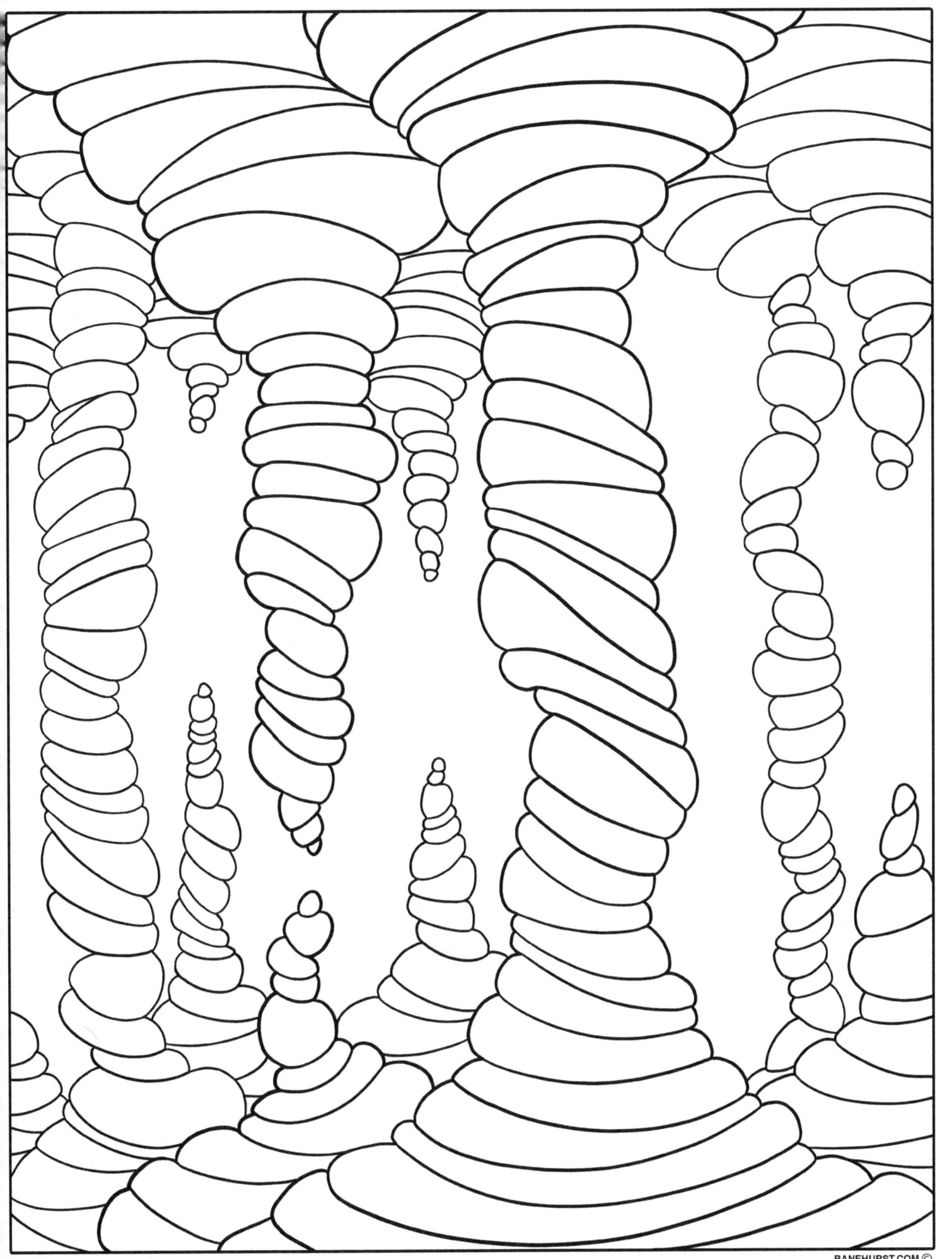

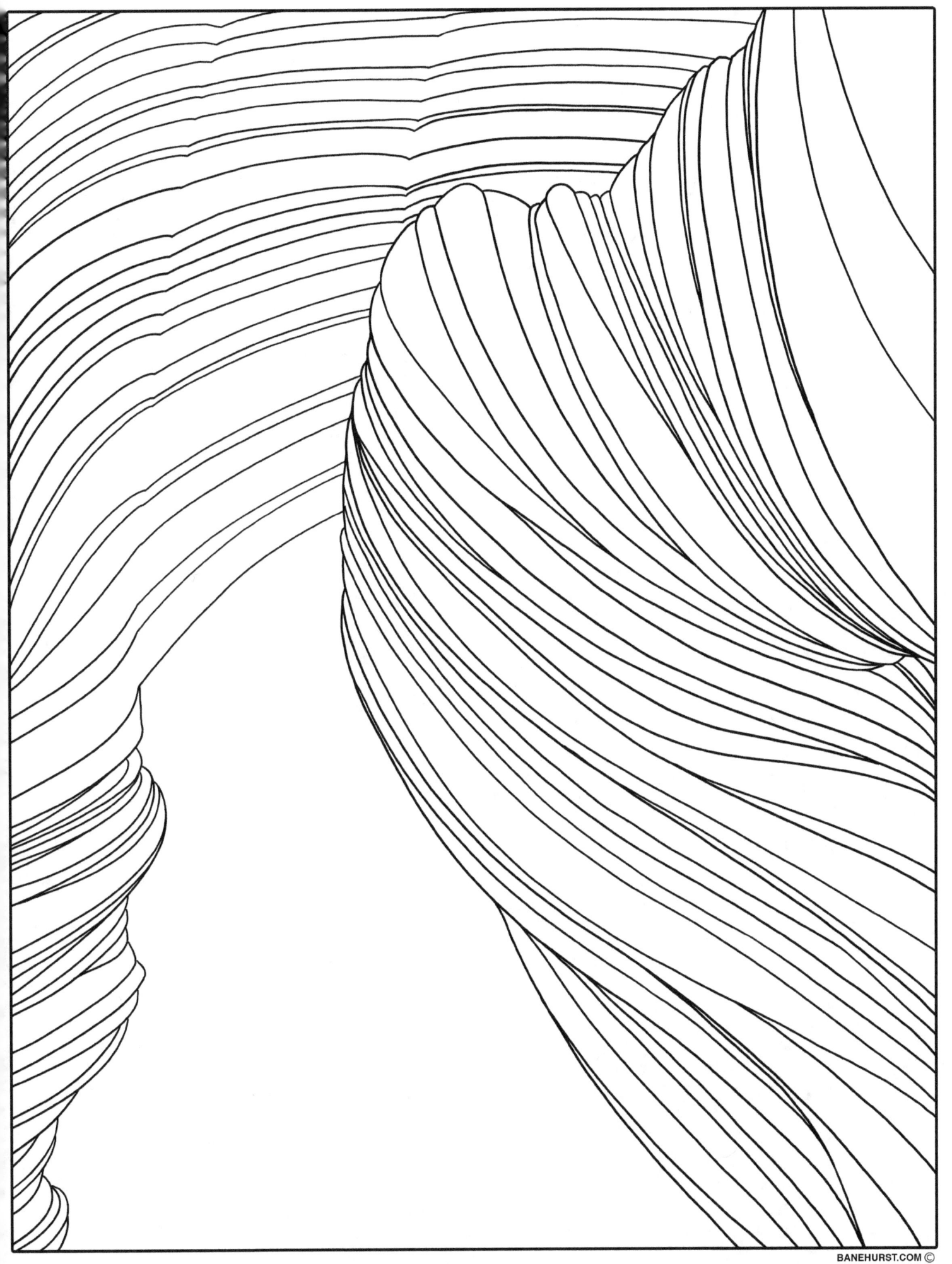

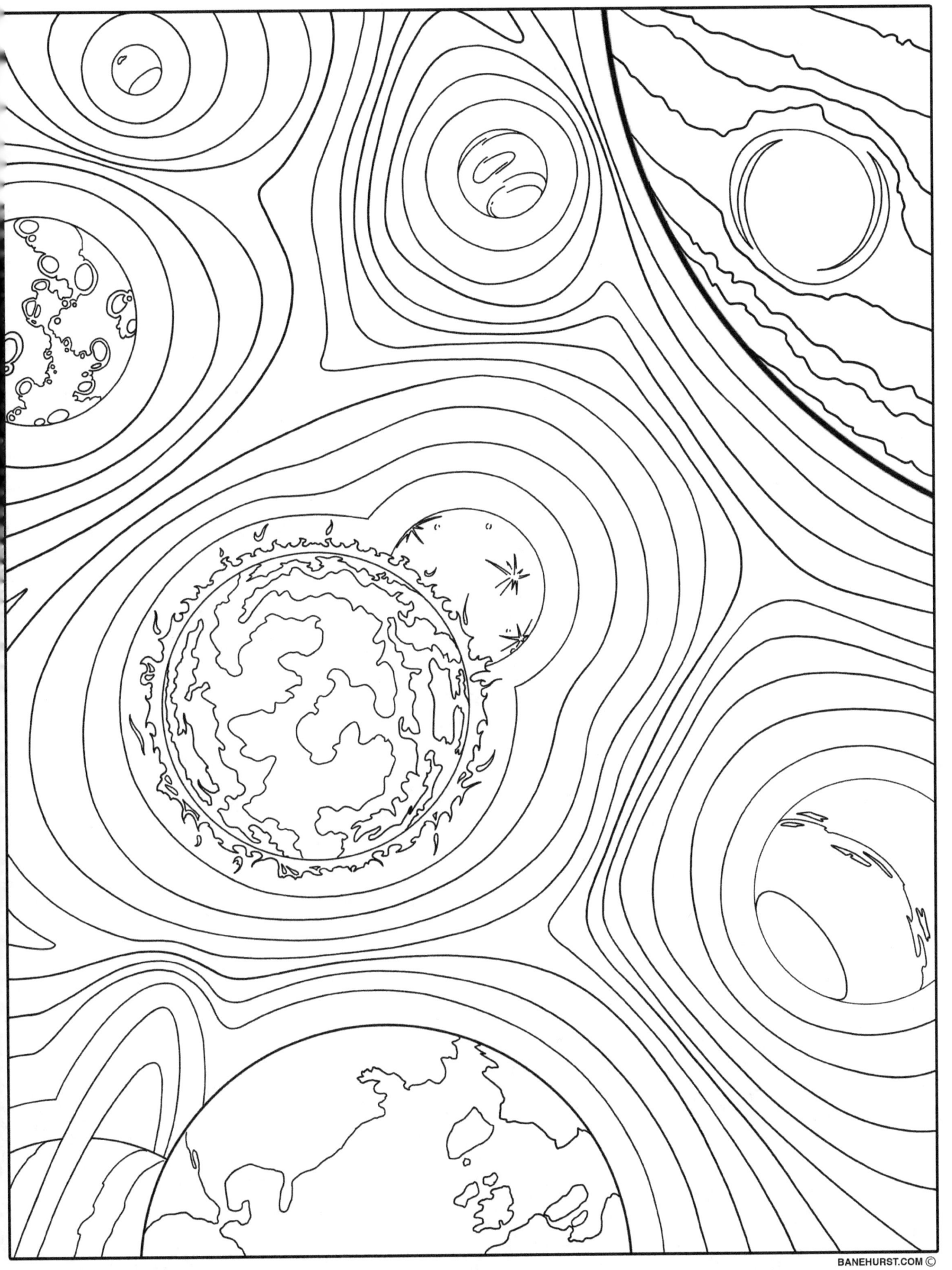

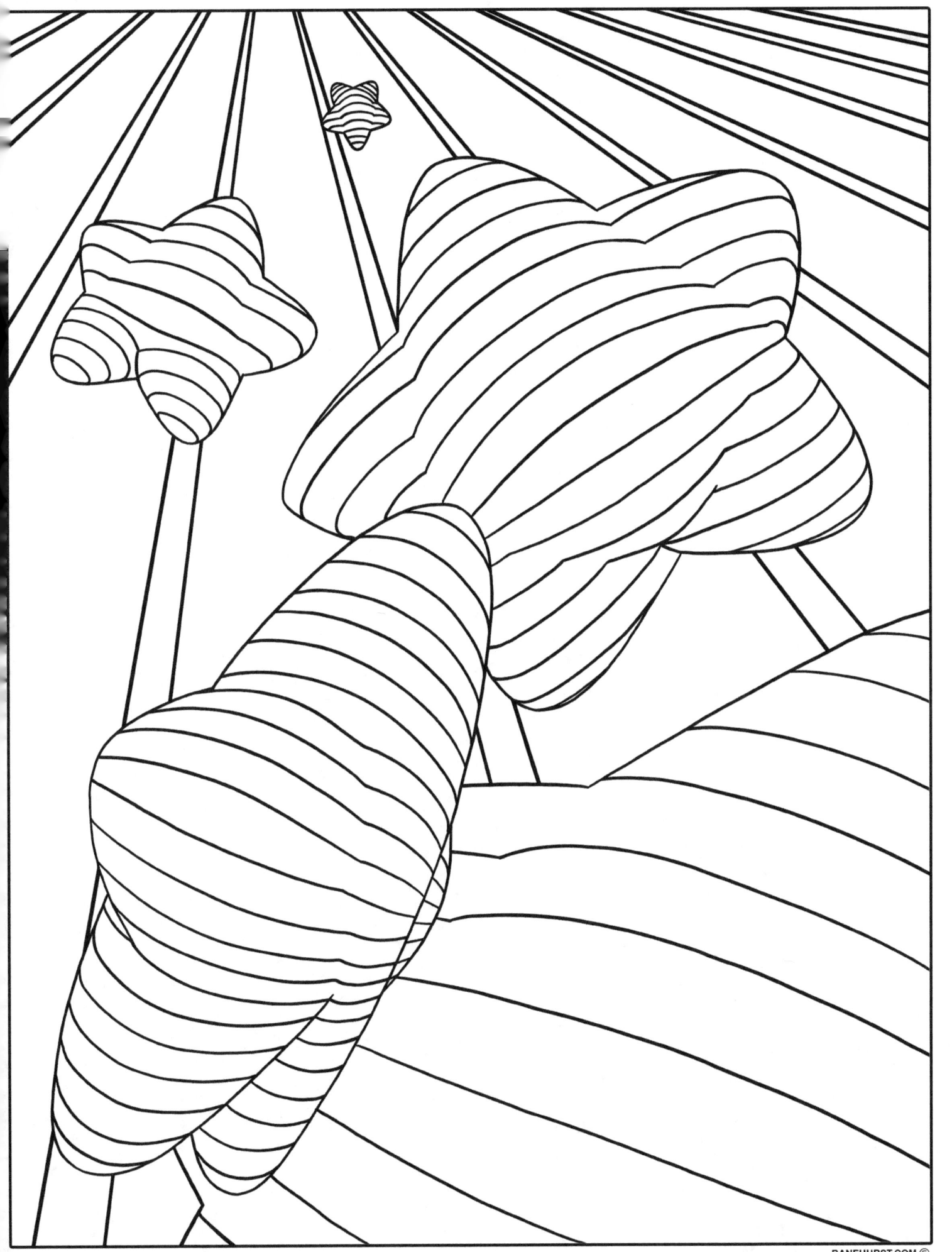

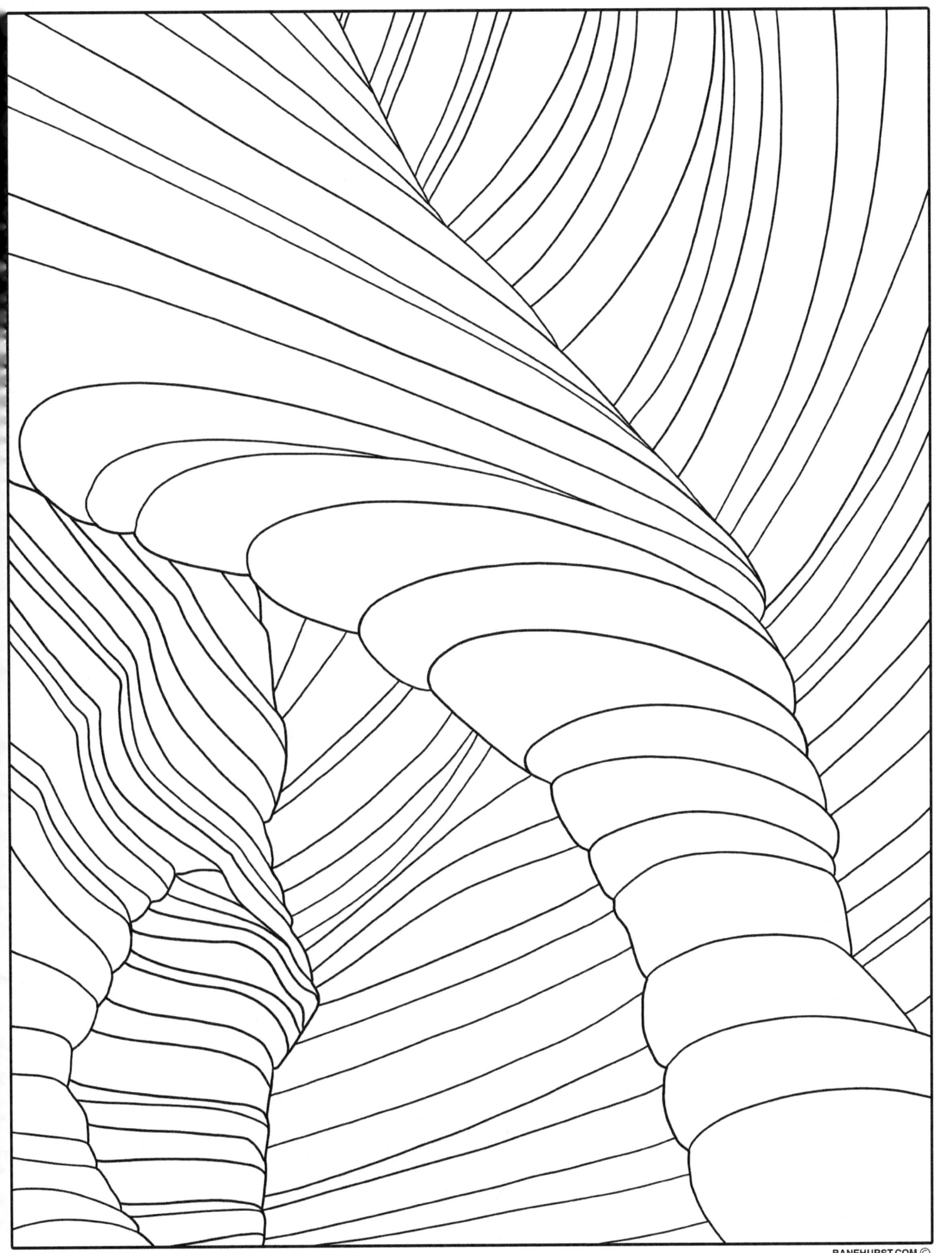

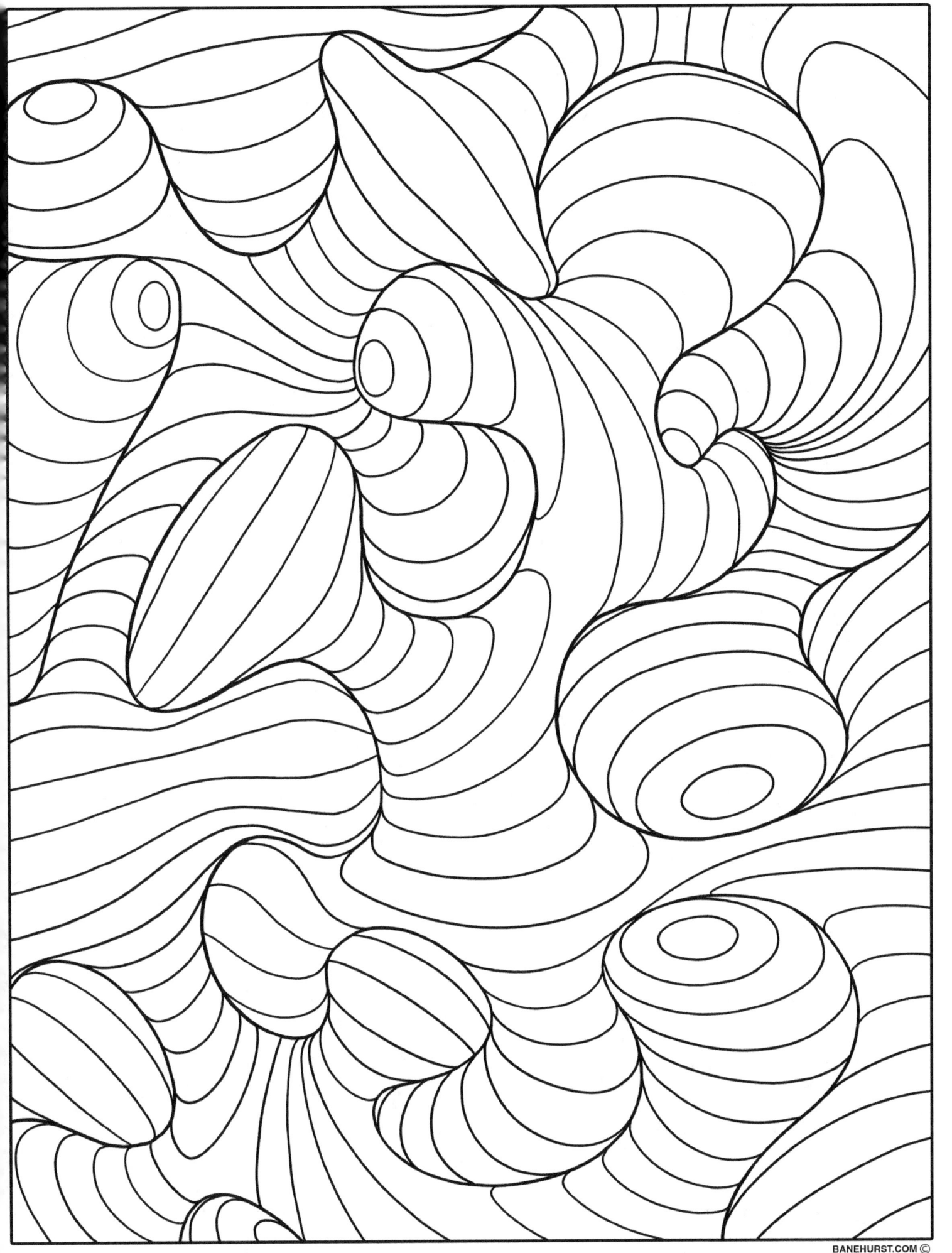

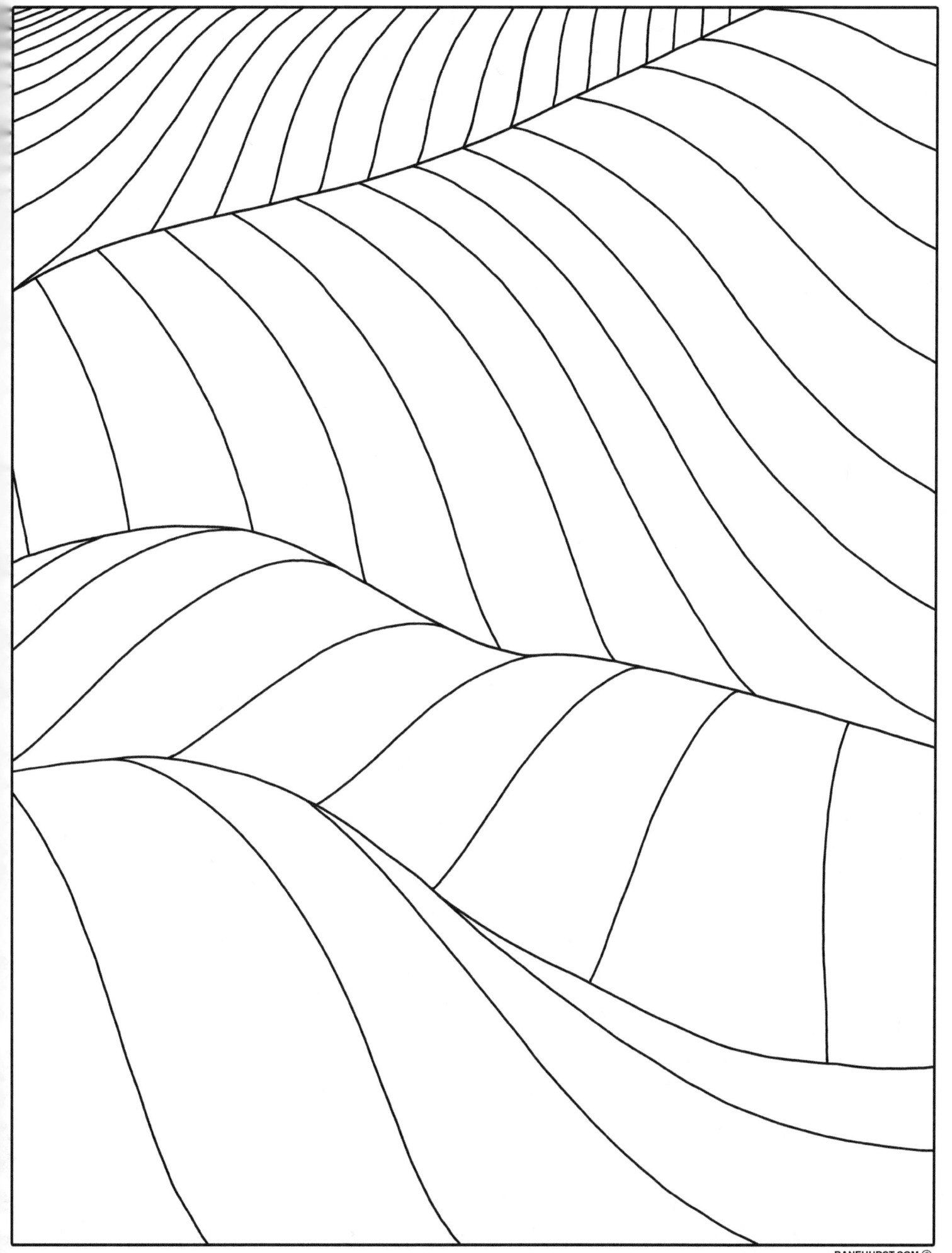

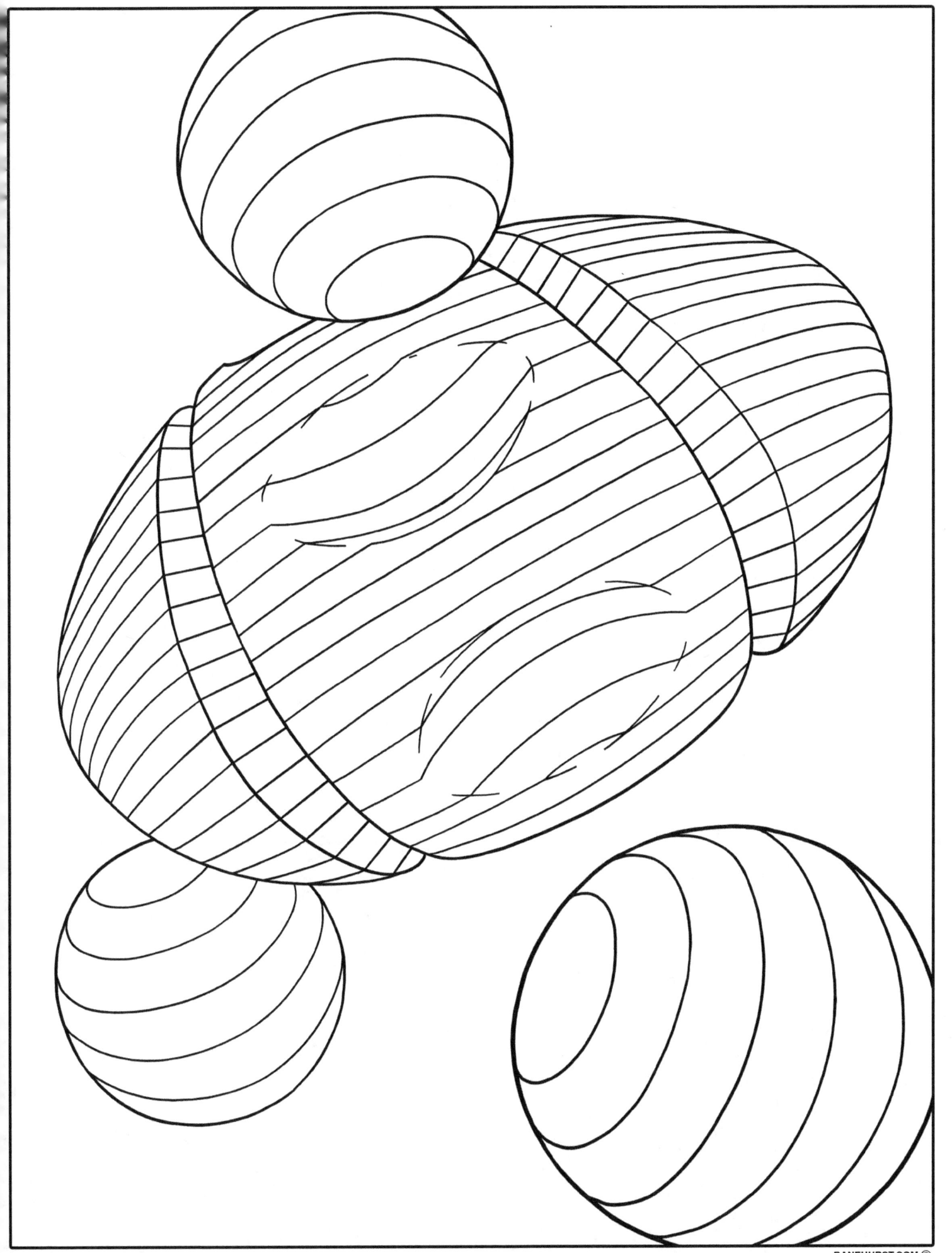

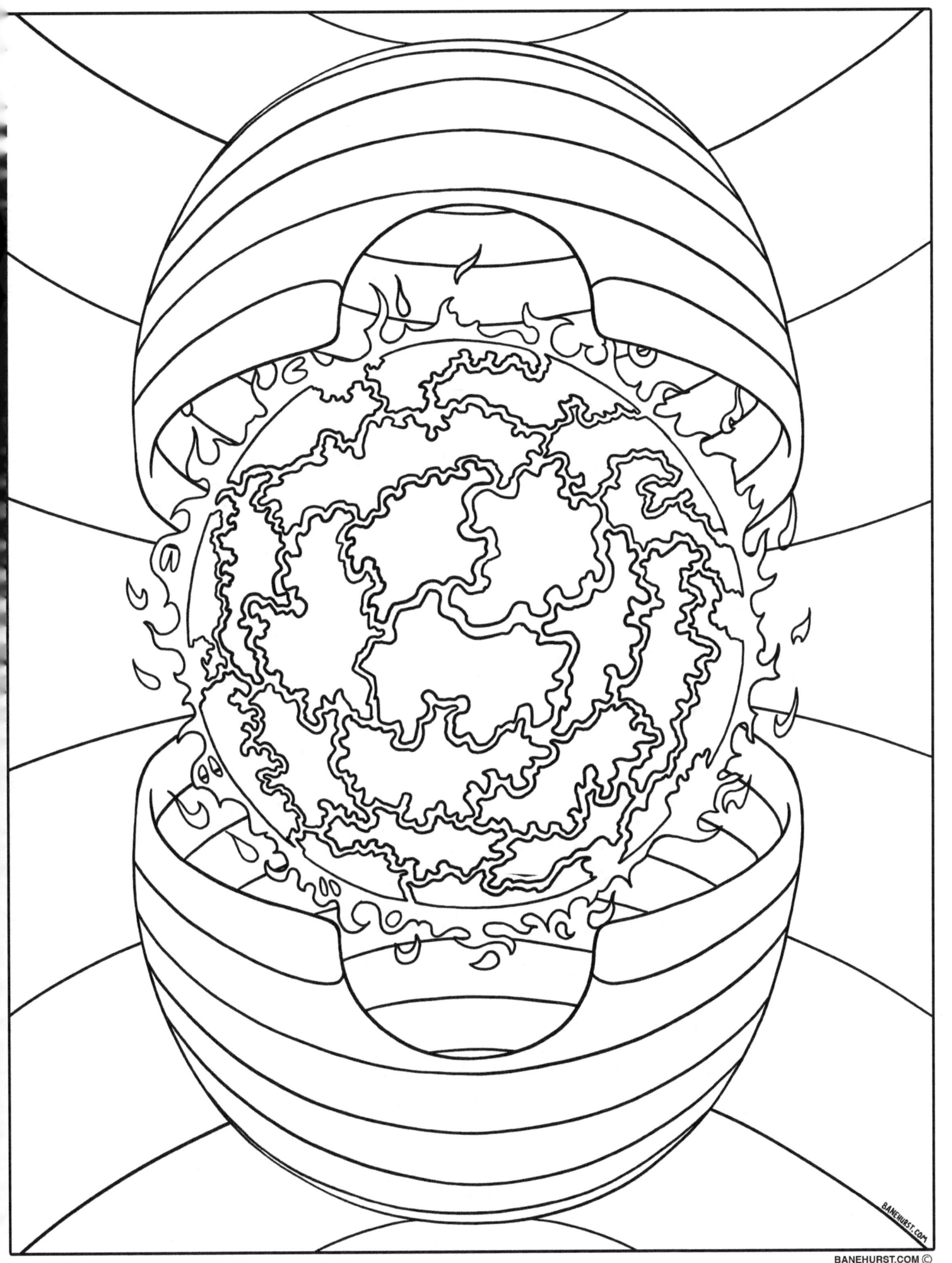

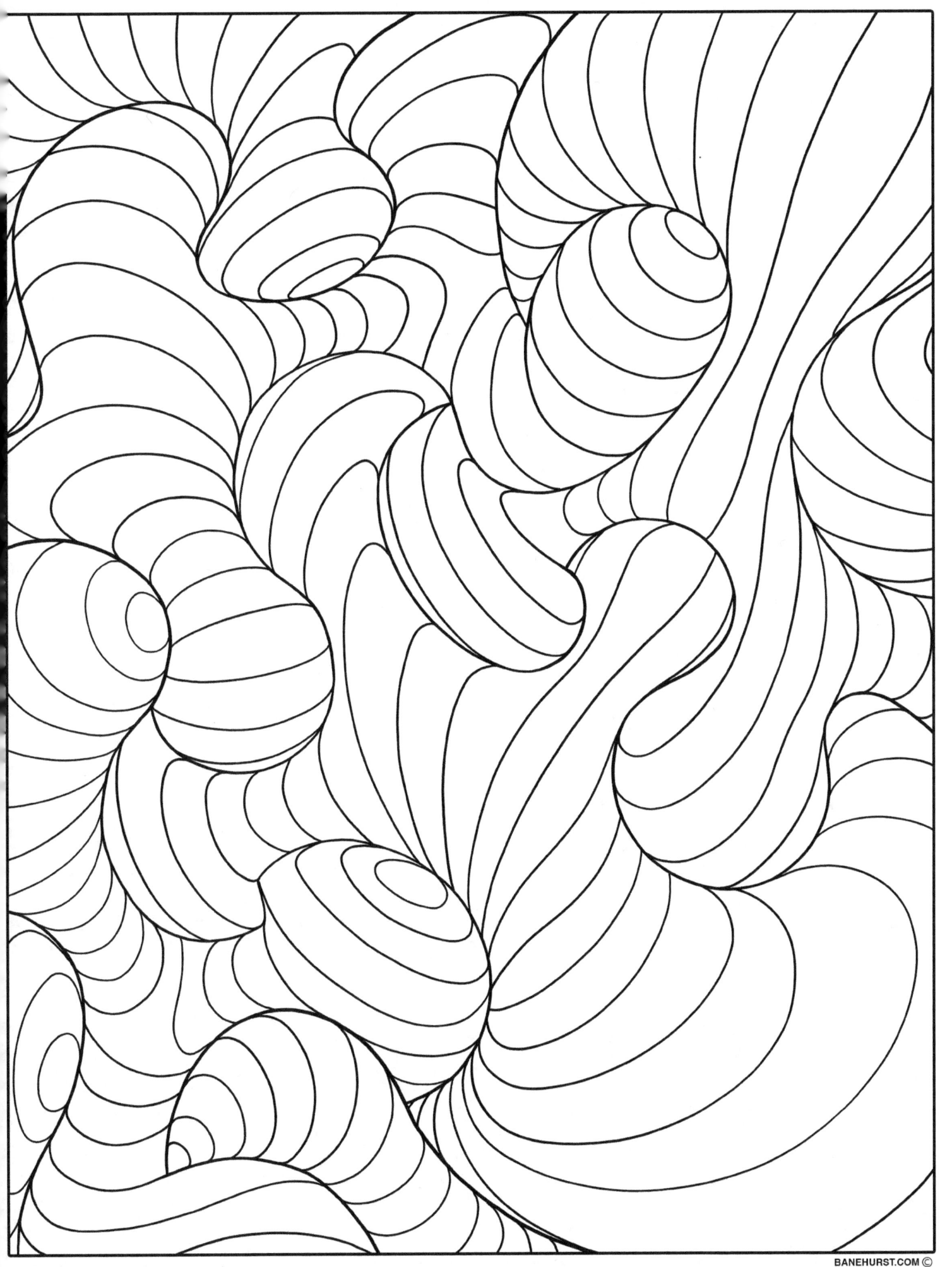

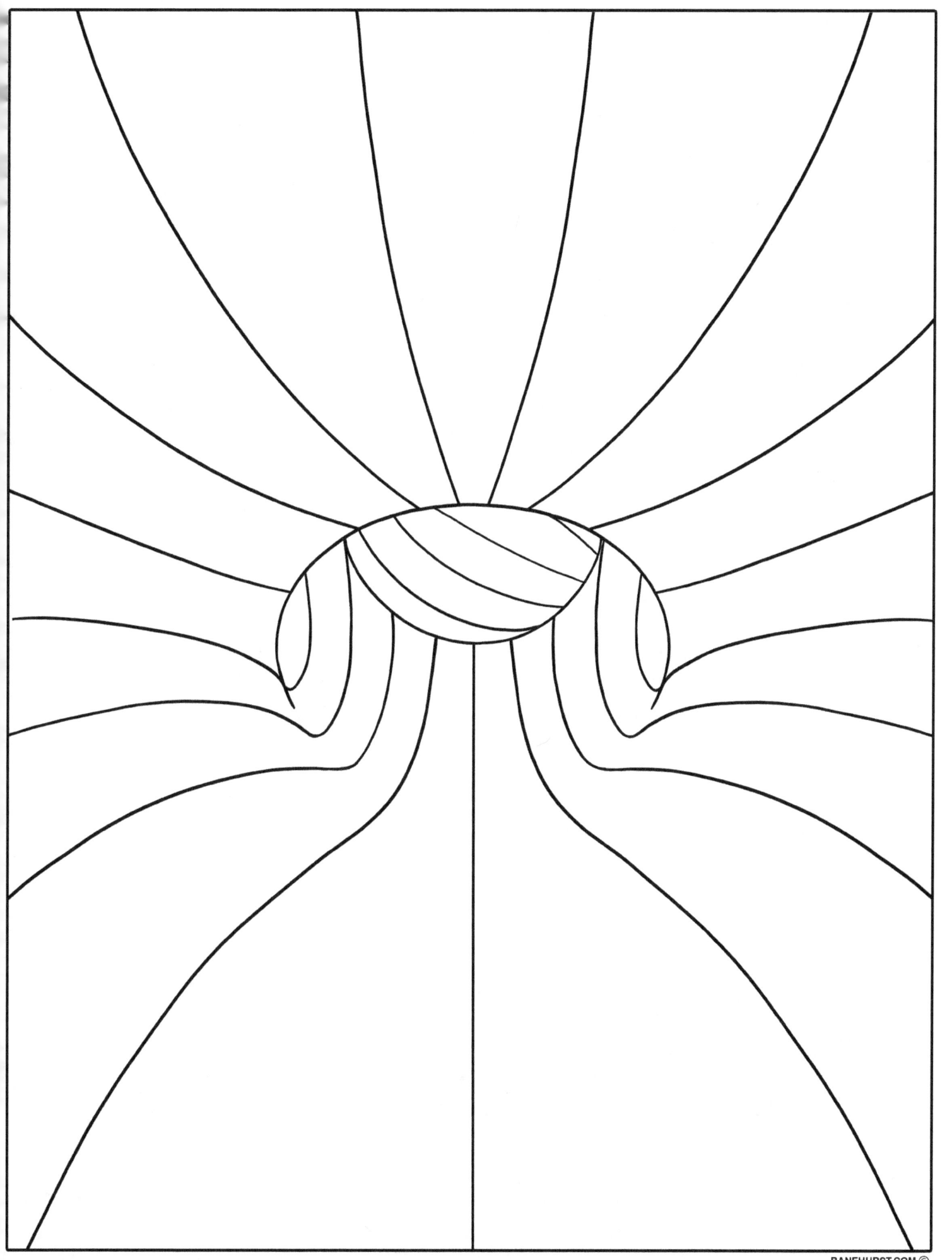

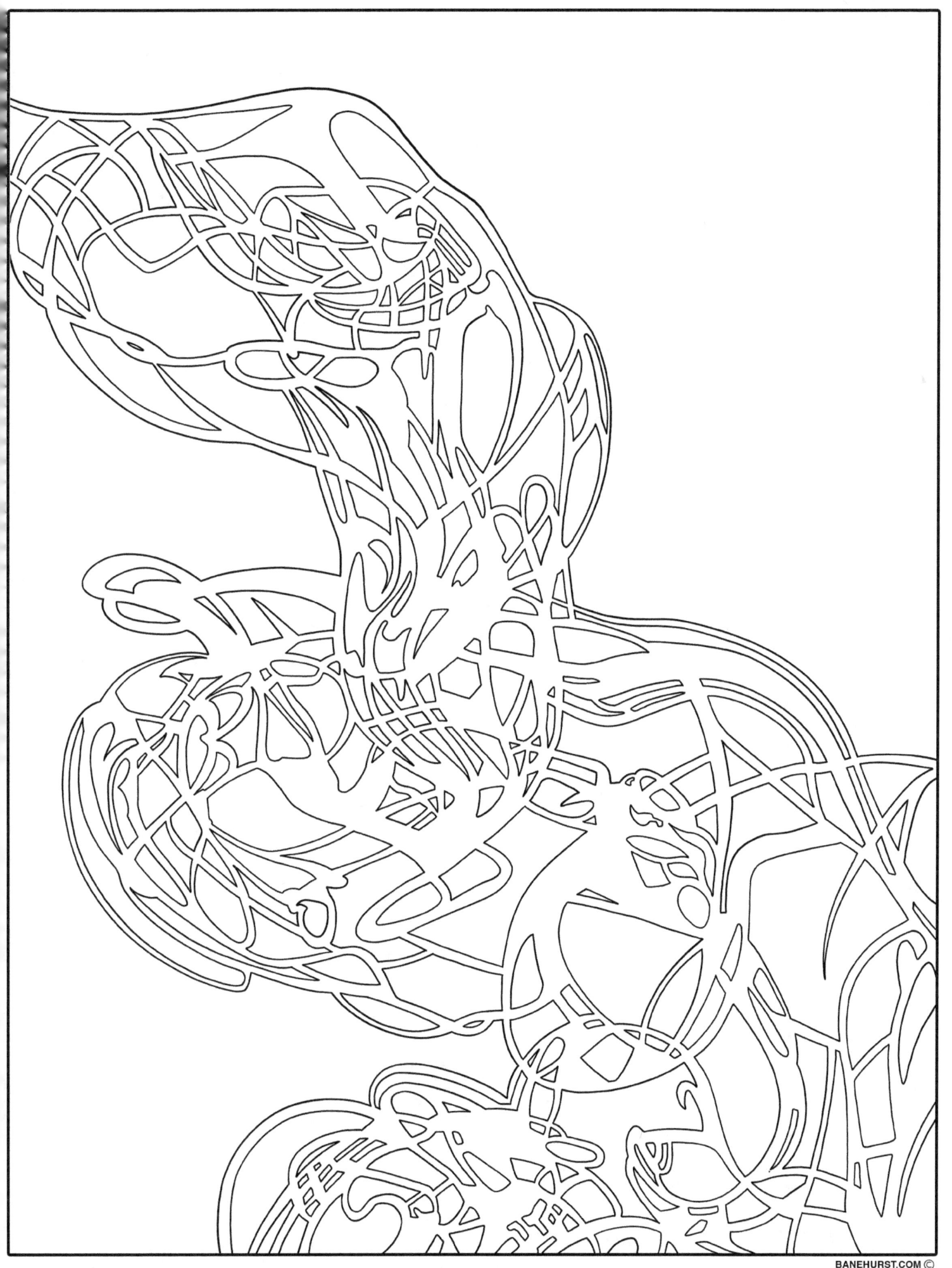

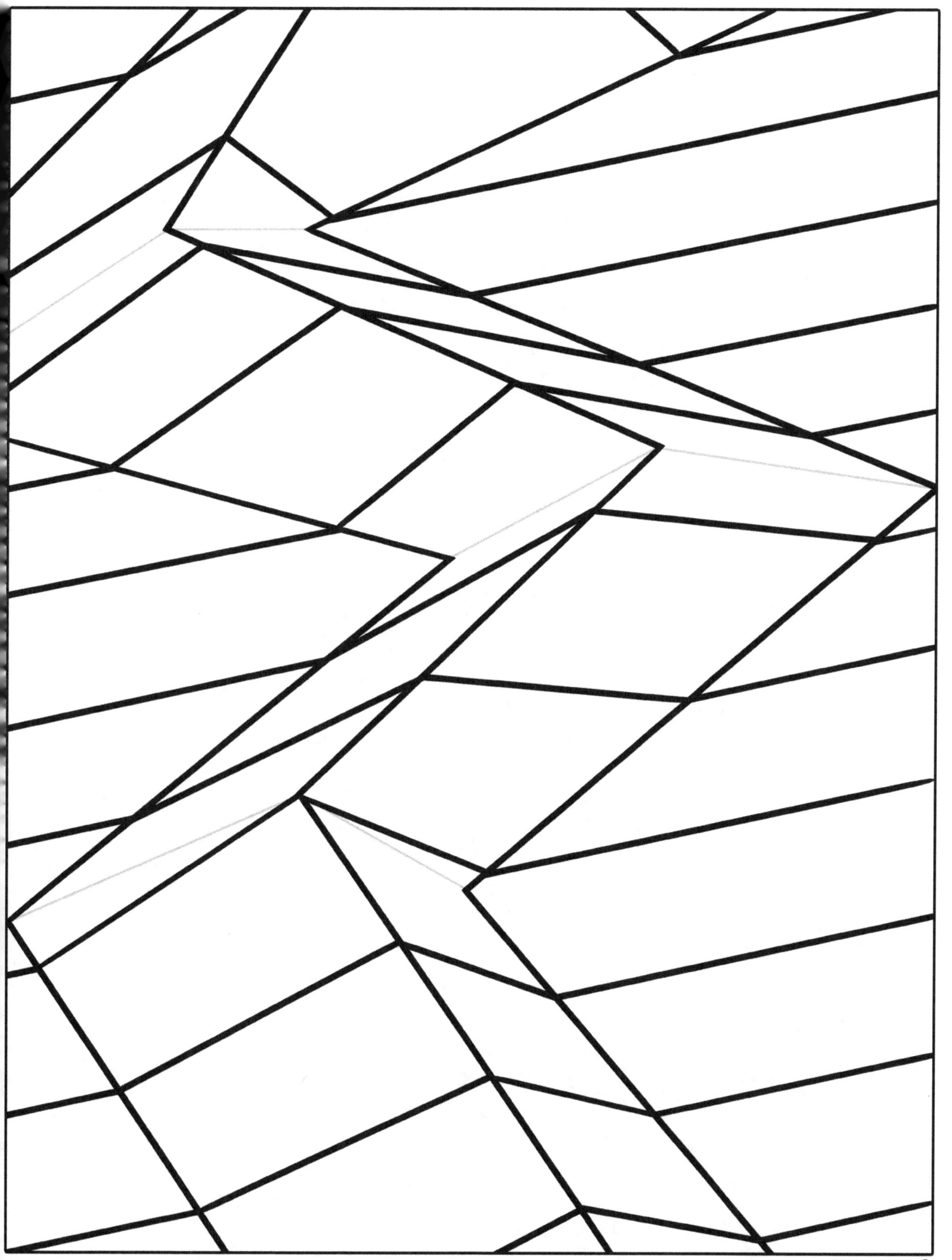

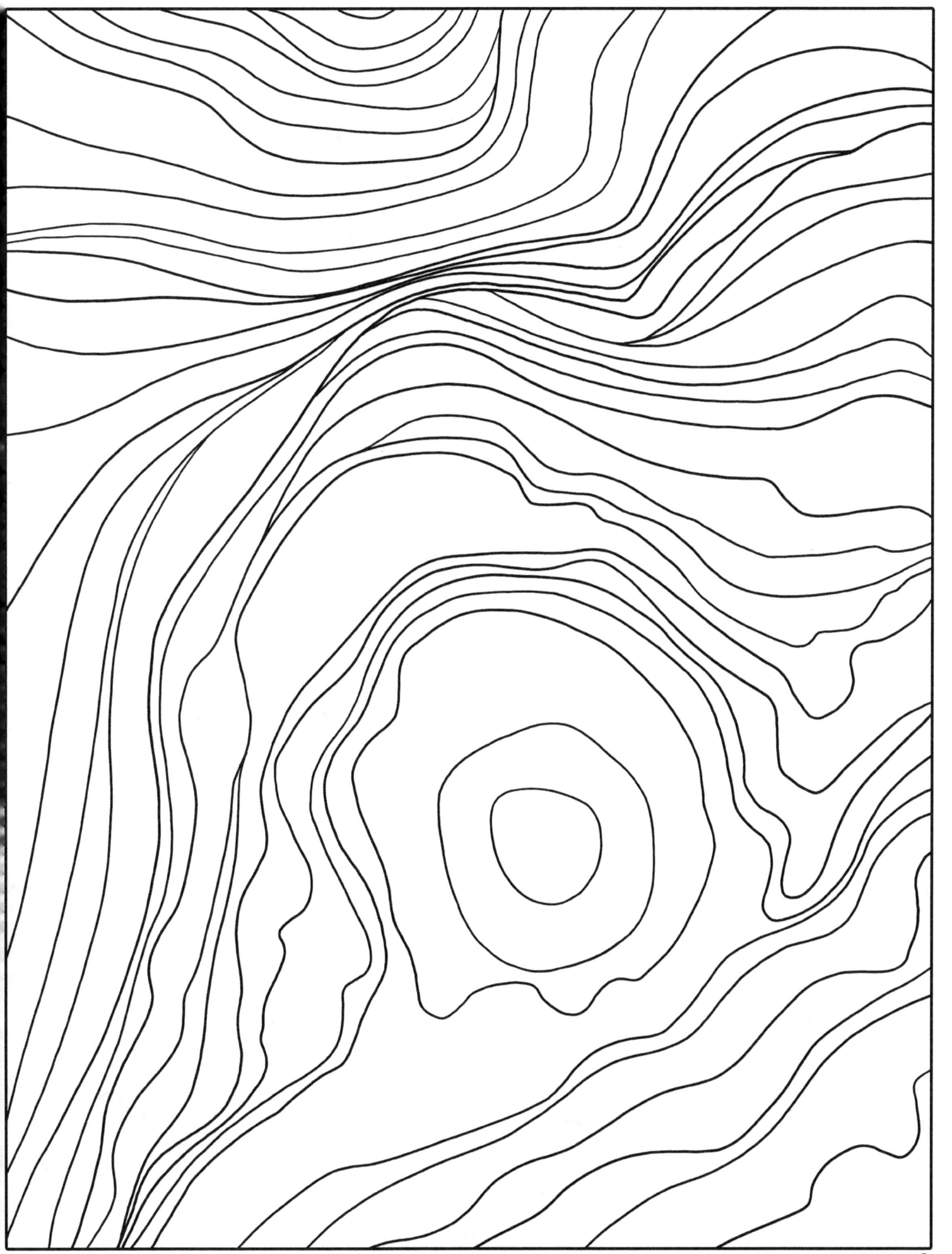

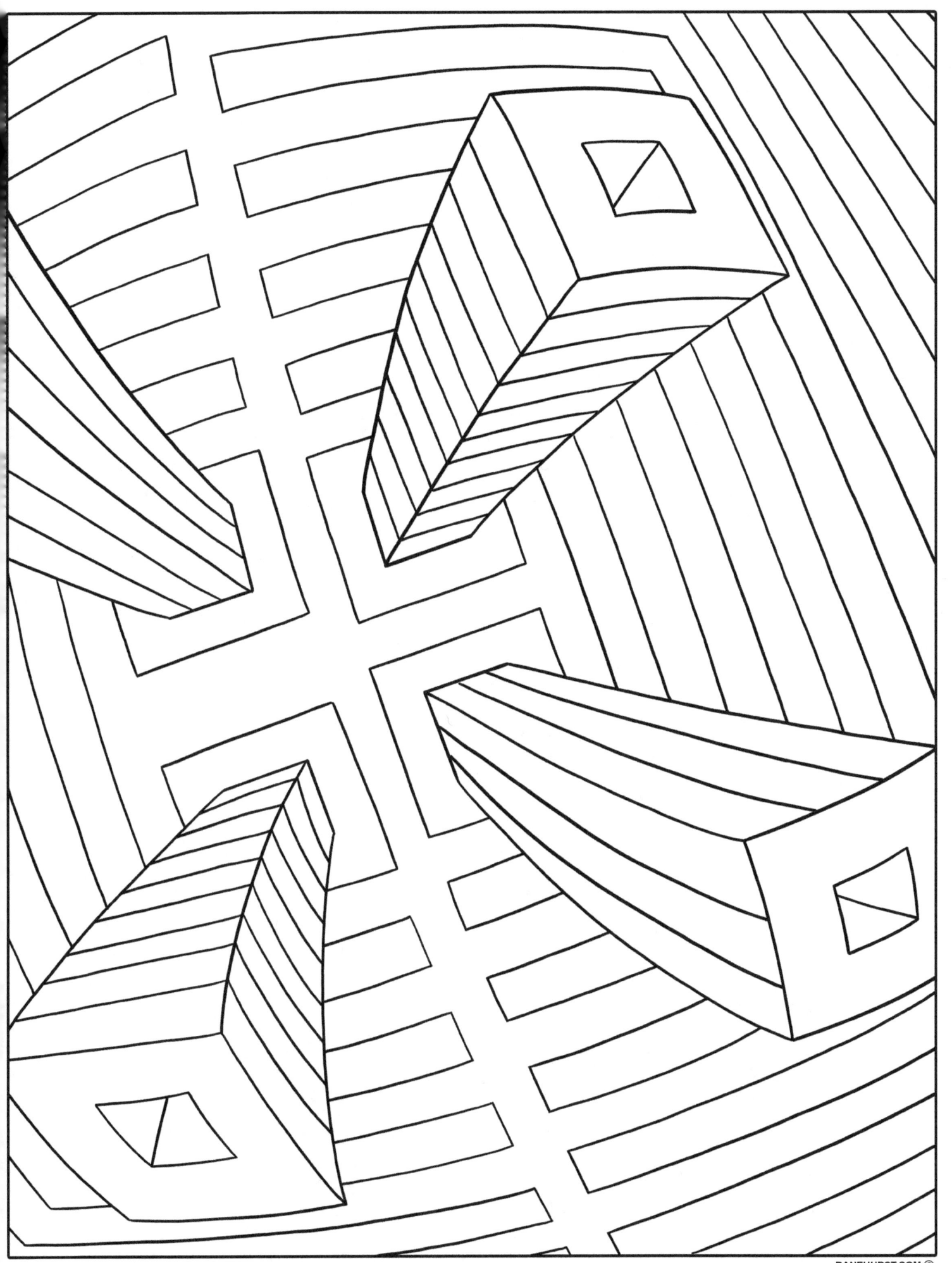

www.ingramcontent.com/pod-product-compliance
Lightning Source LLC
Chambersburg PA
CBHW062234220526
45471CB00009B/3471